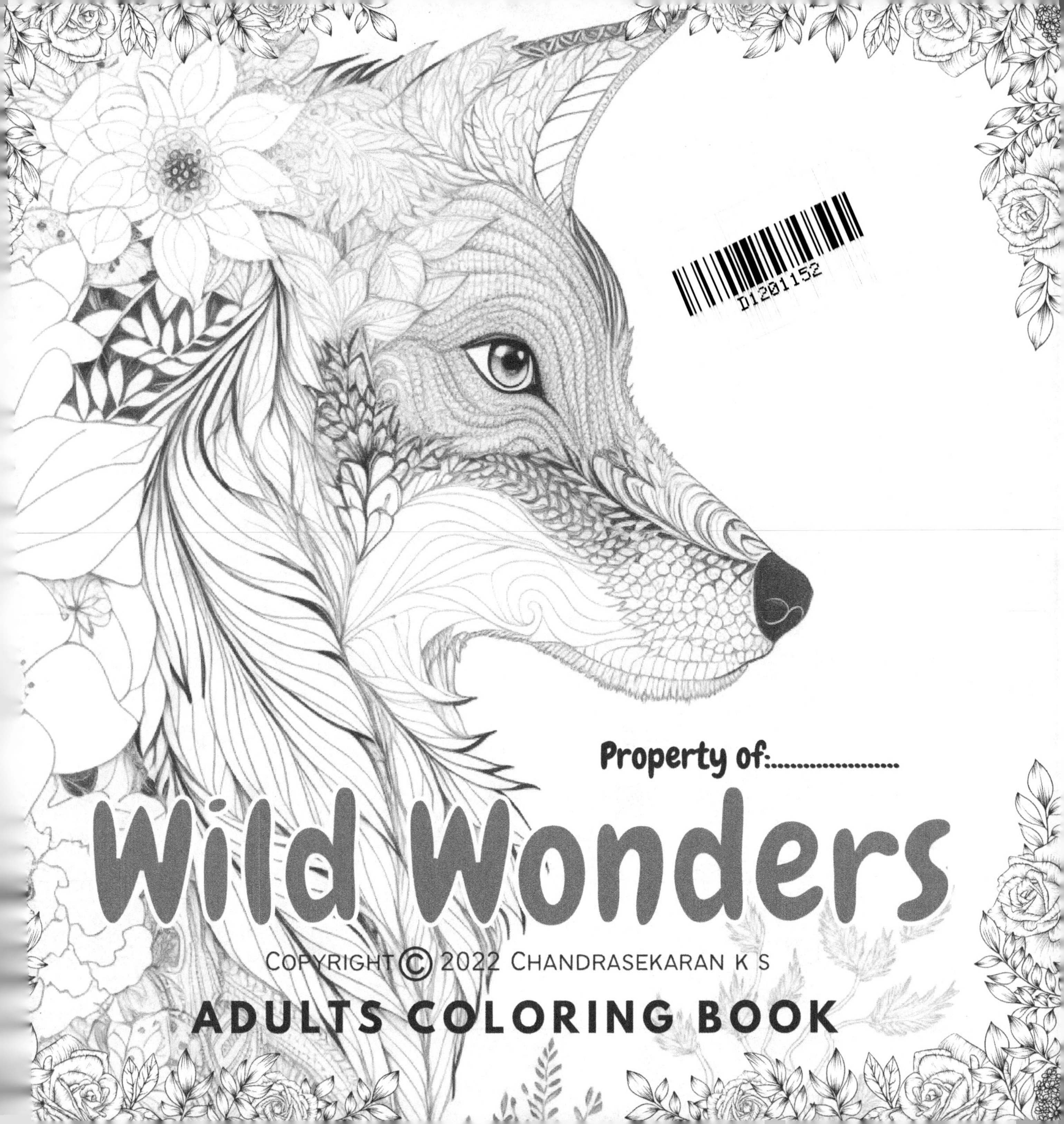

Property of:...................

Wild Wonders

ADULTS COLORING BOOK

Printed in the USA.

First Edition, January 2023

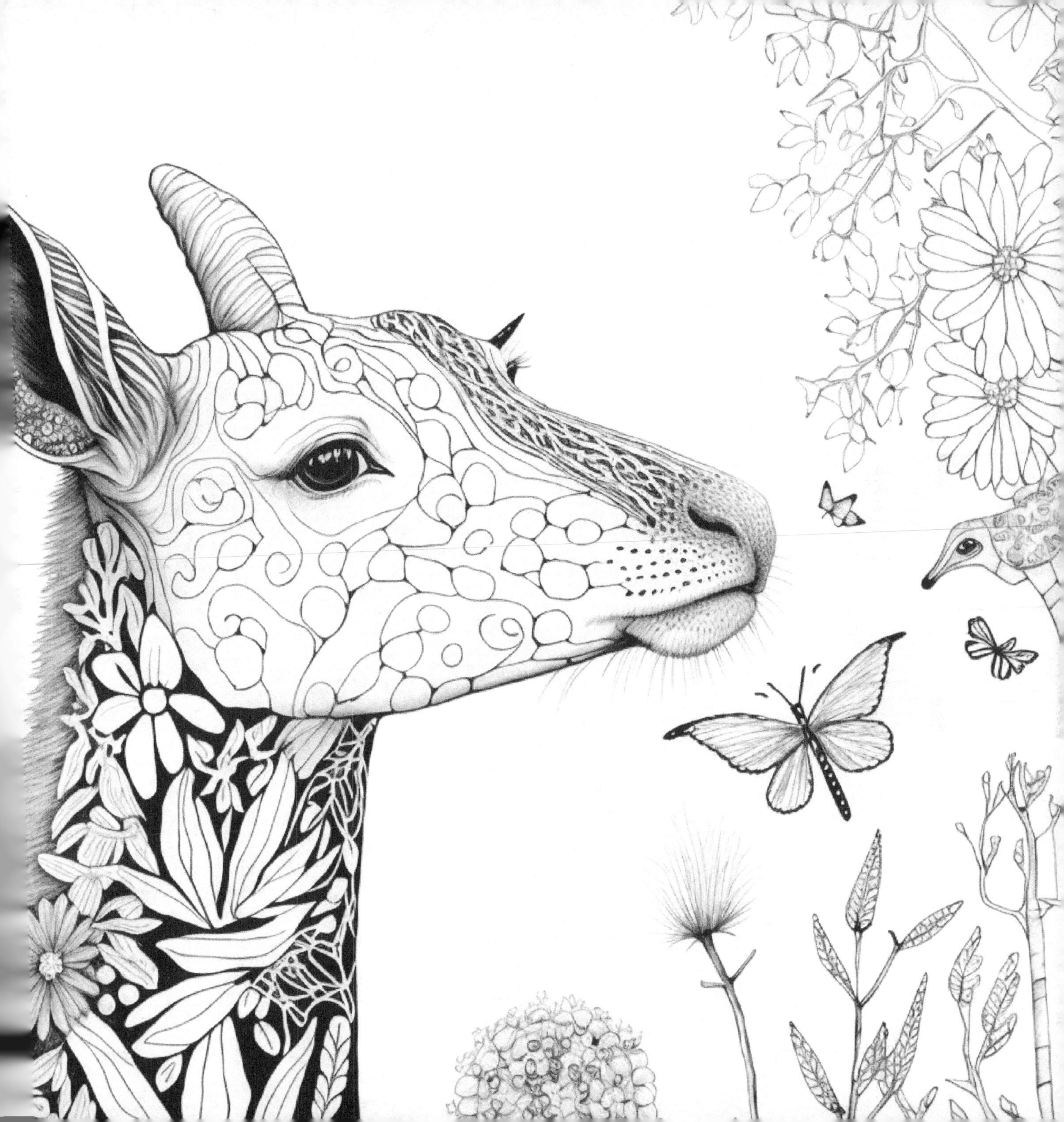

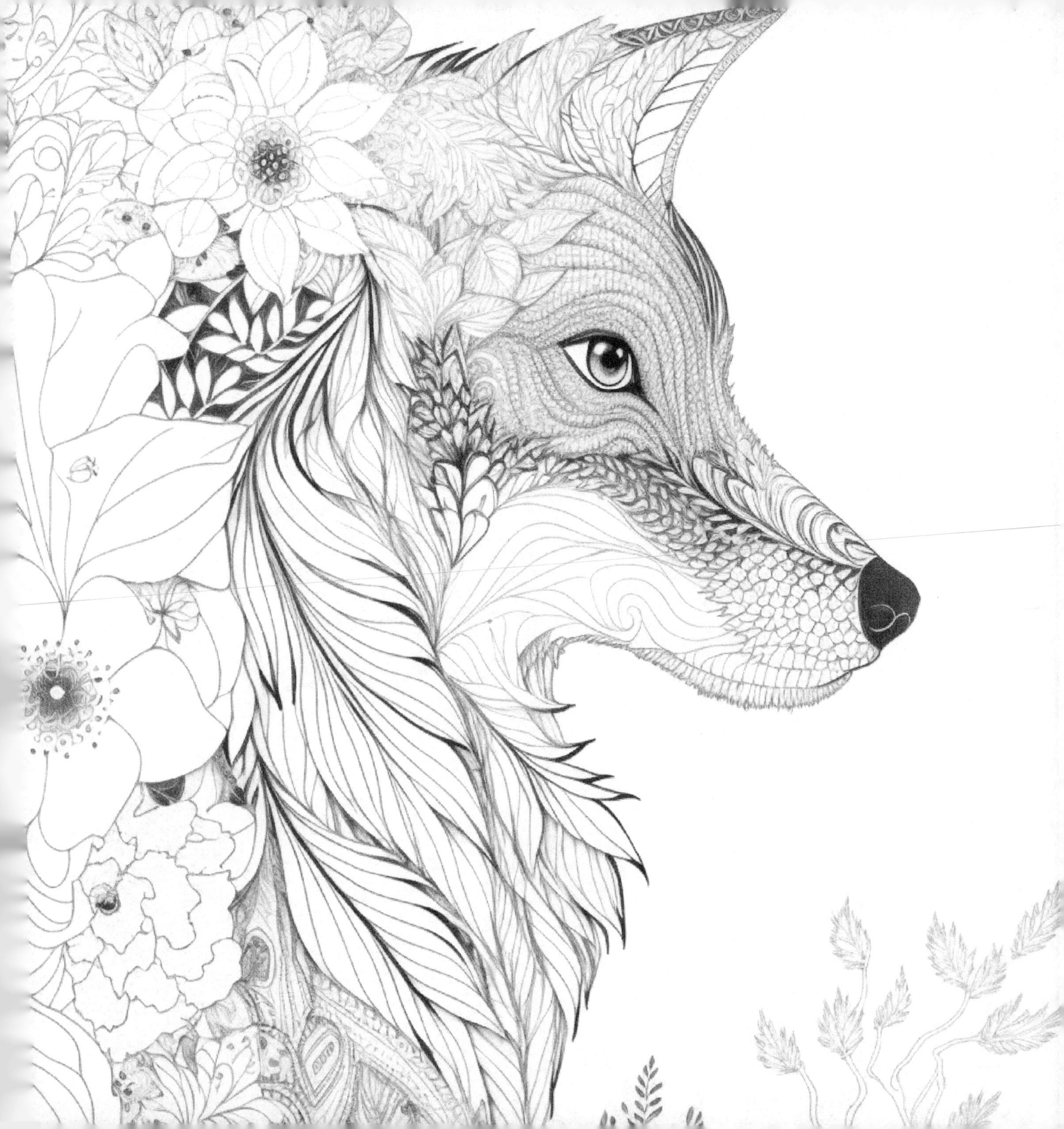

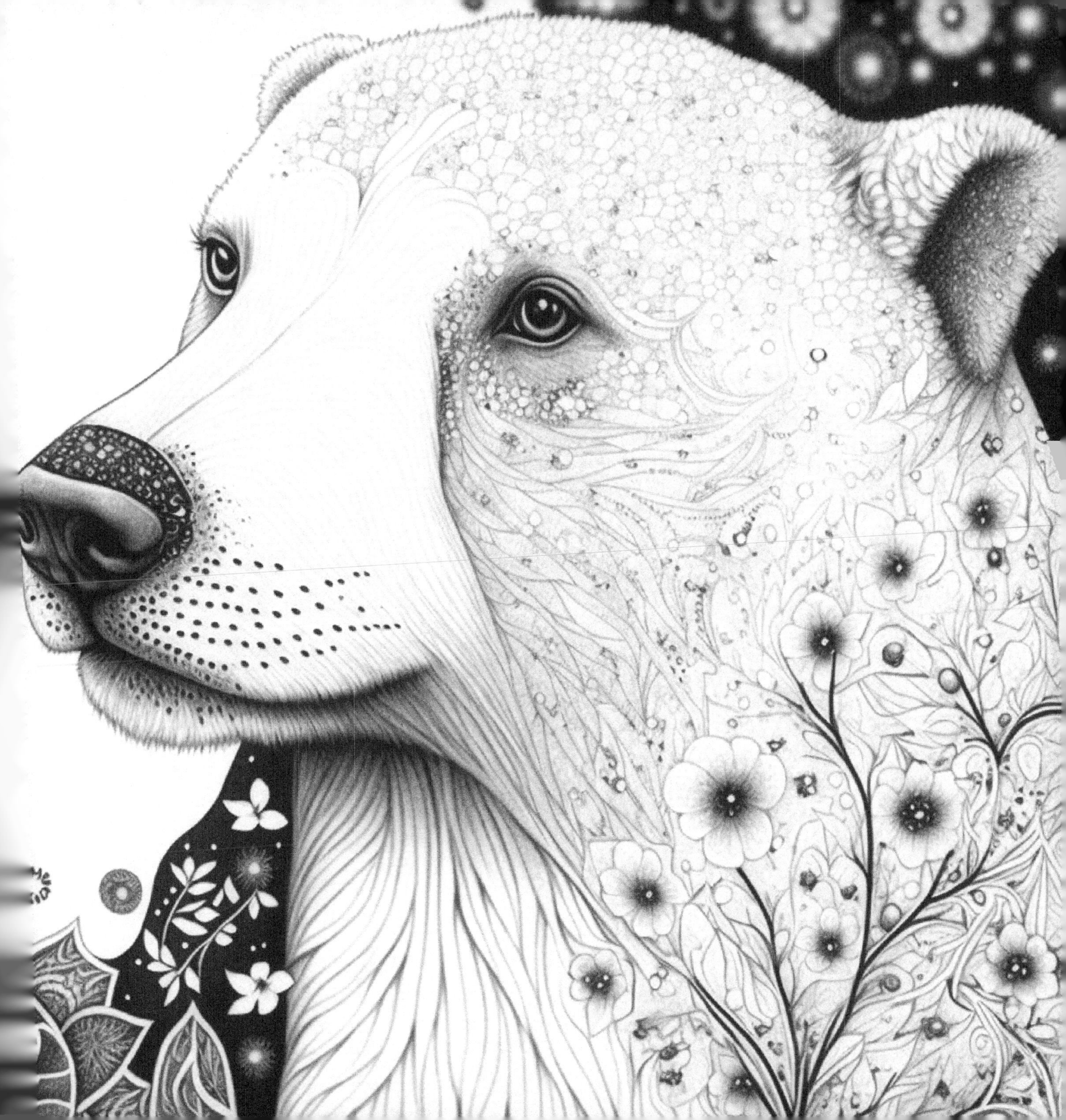

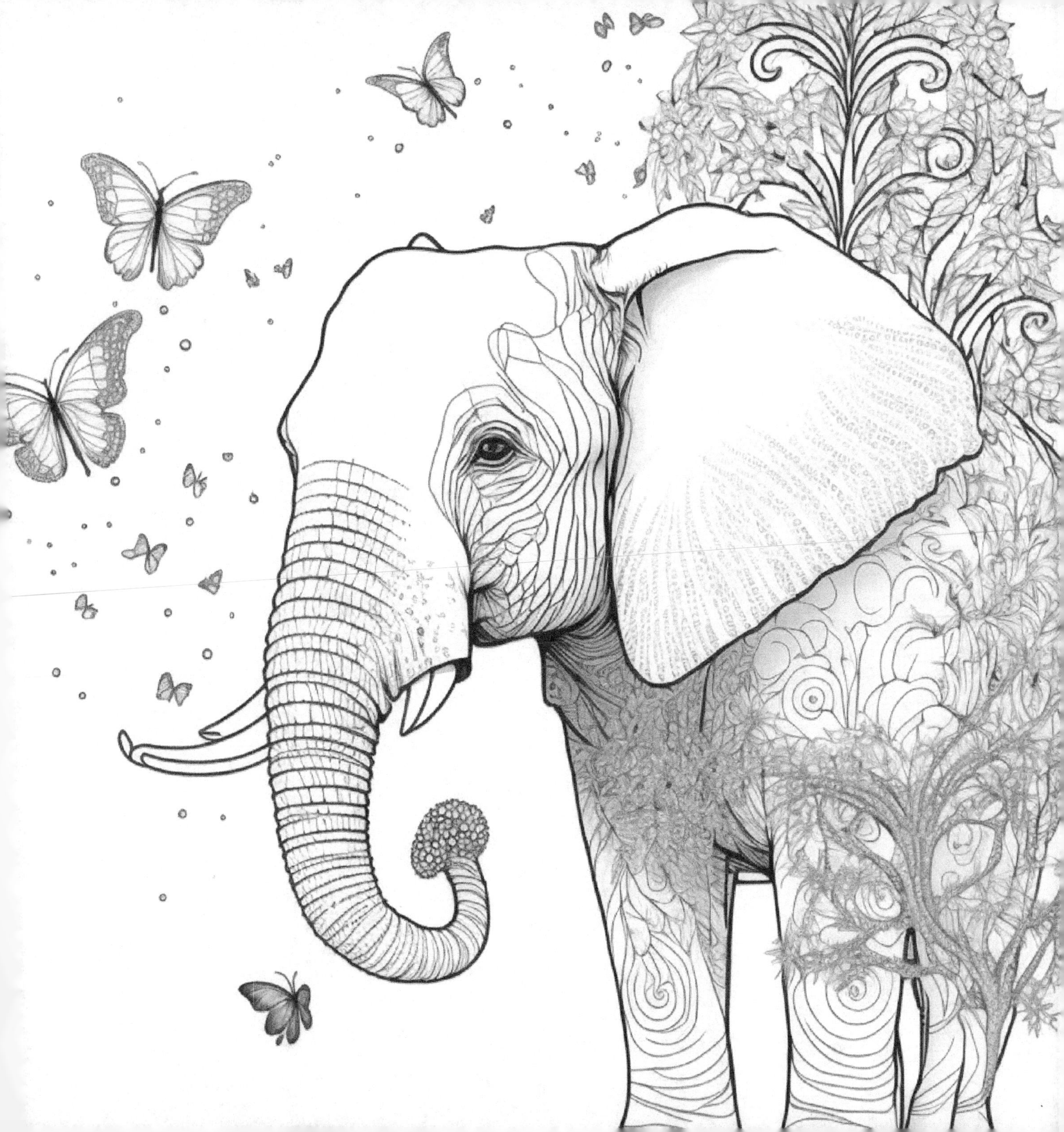

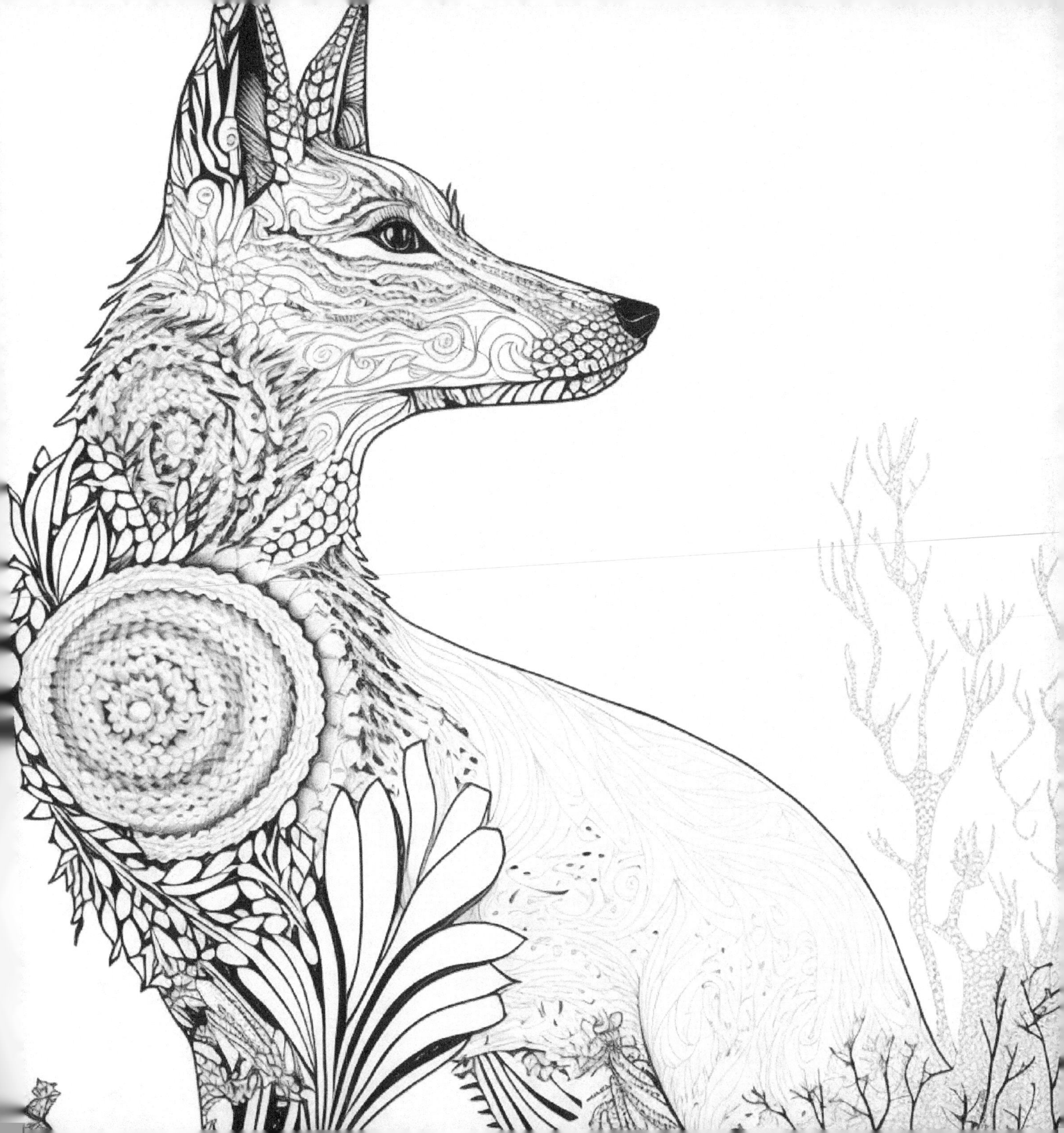

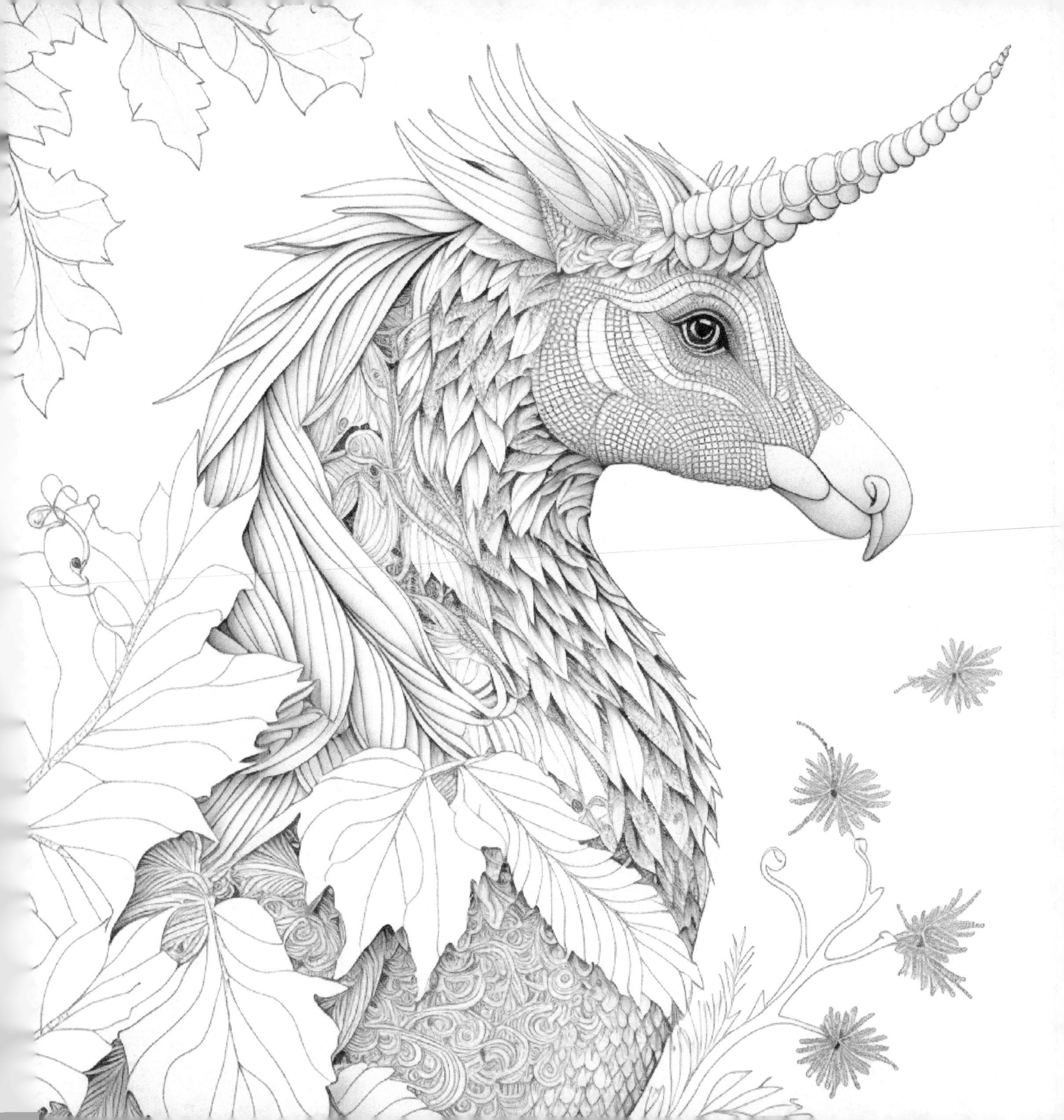

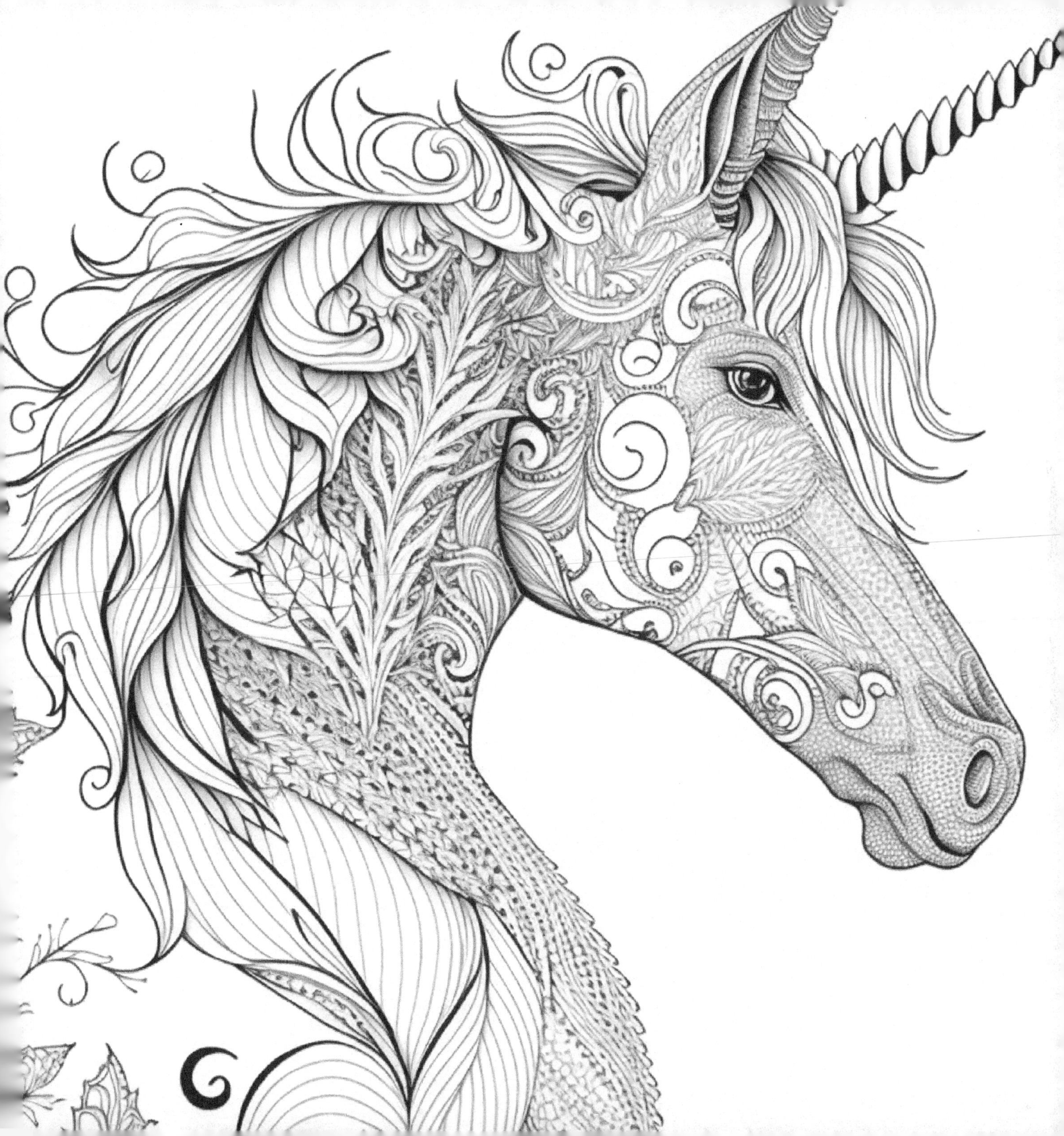

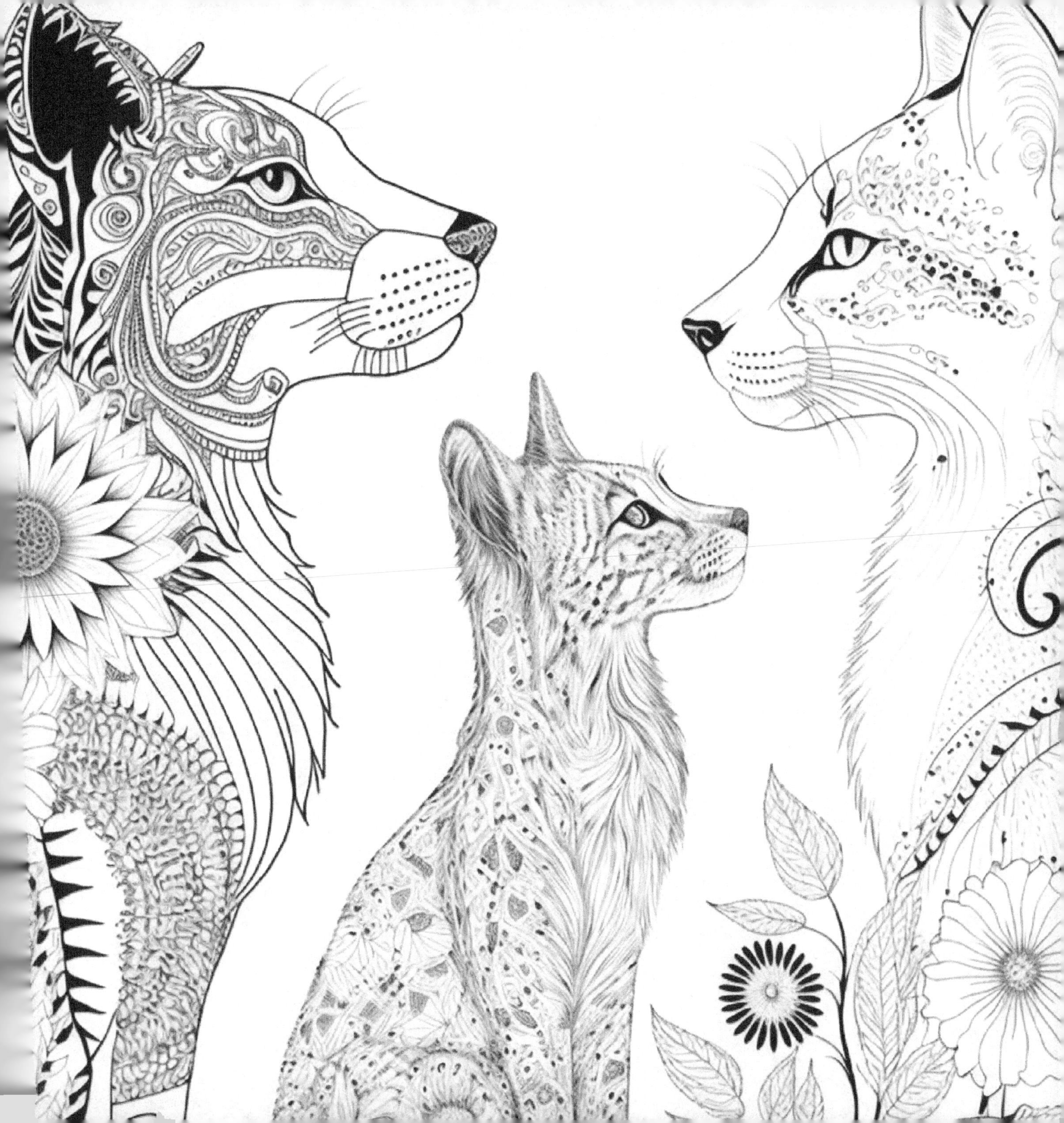

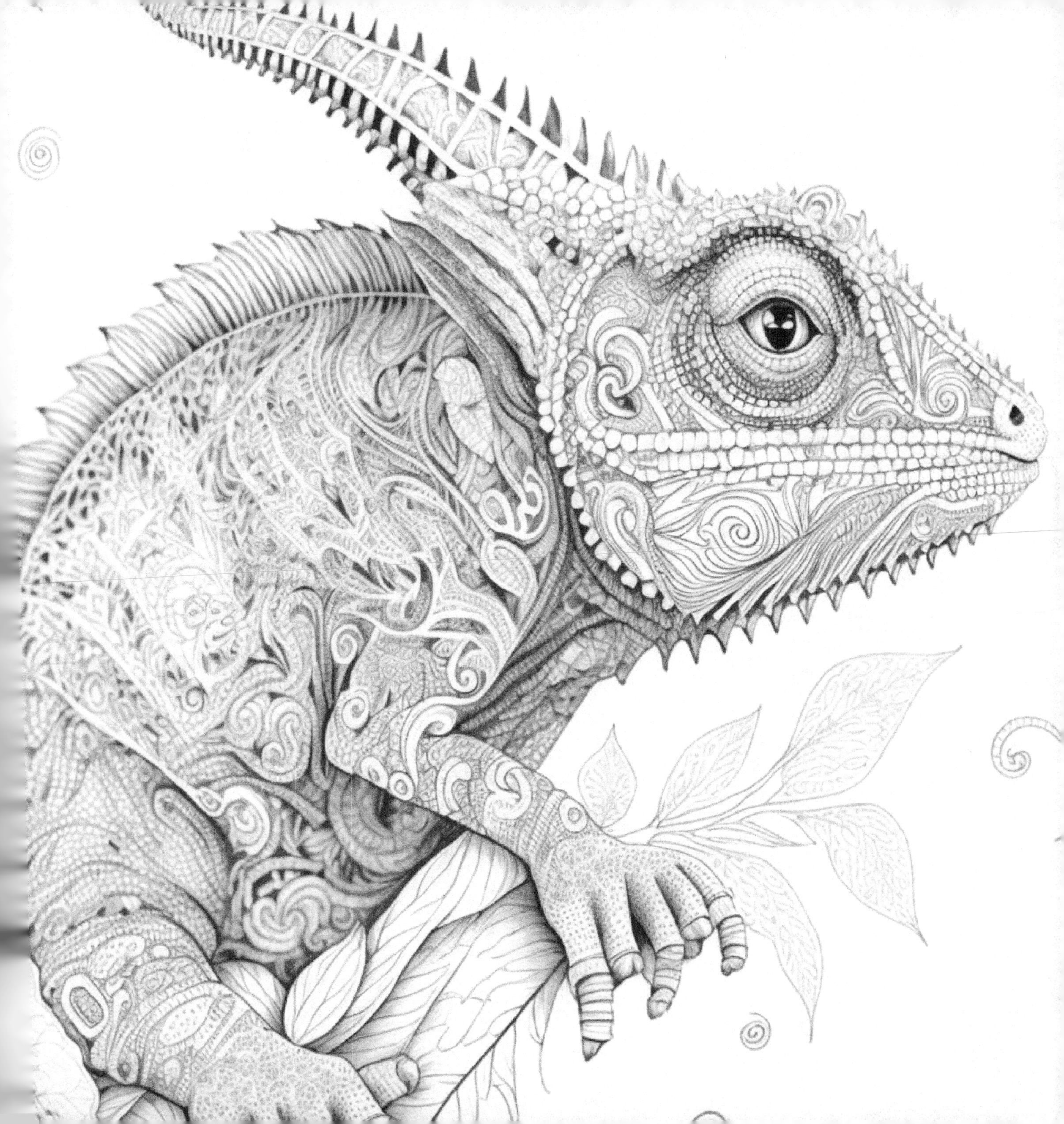

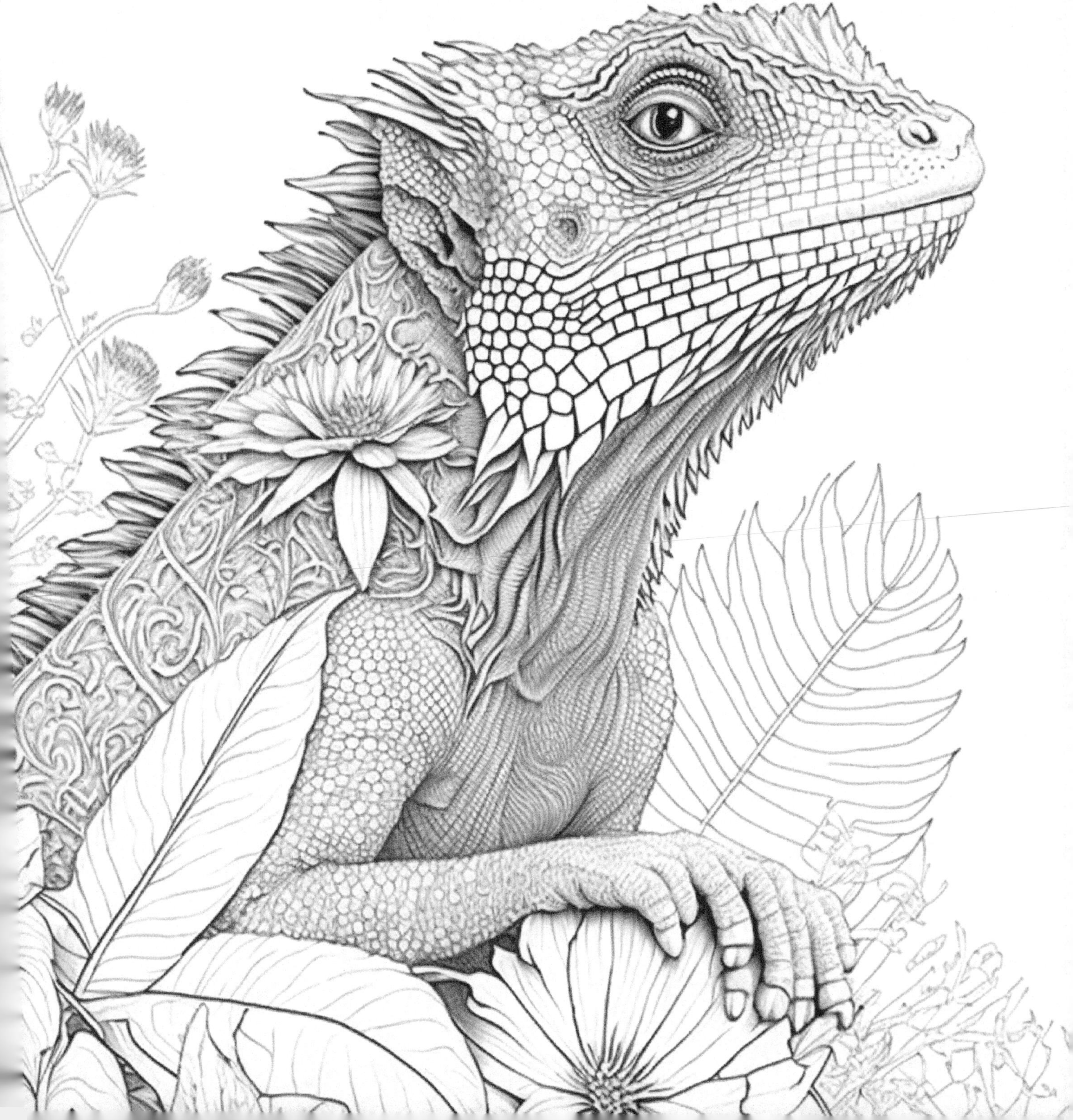

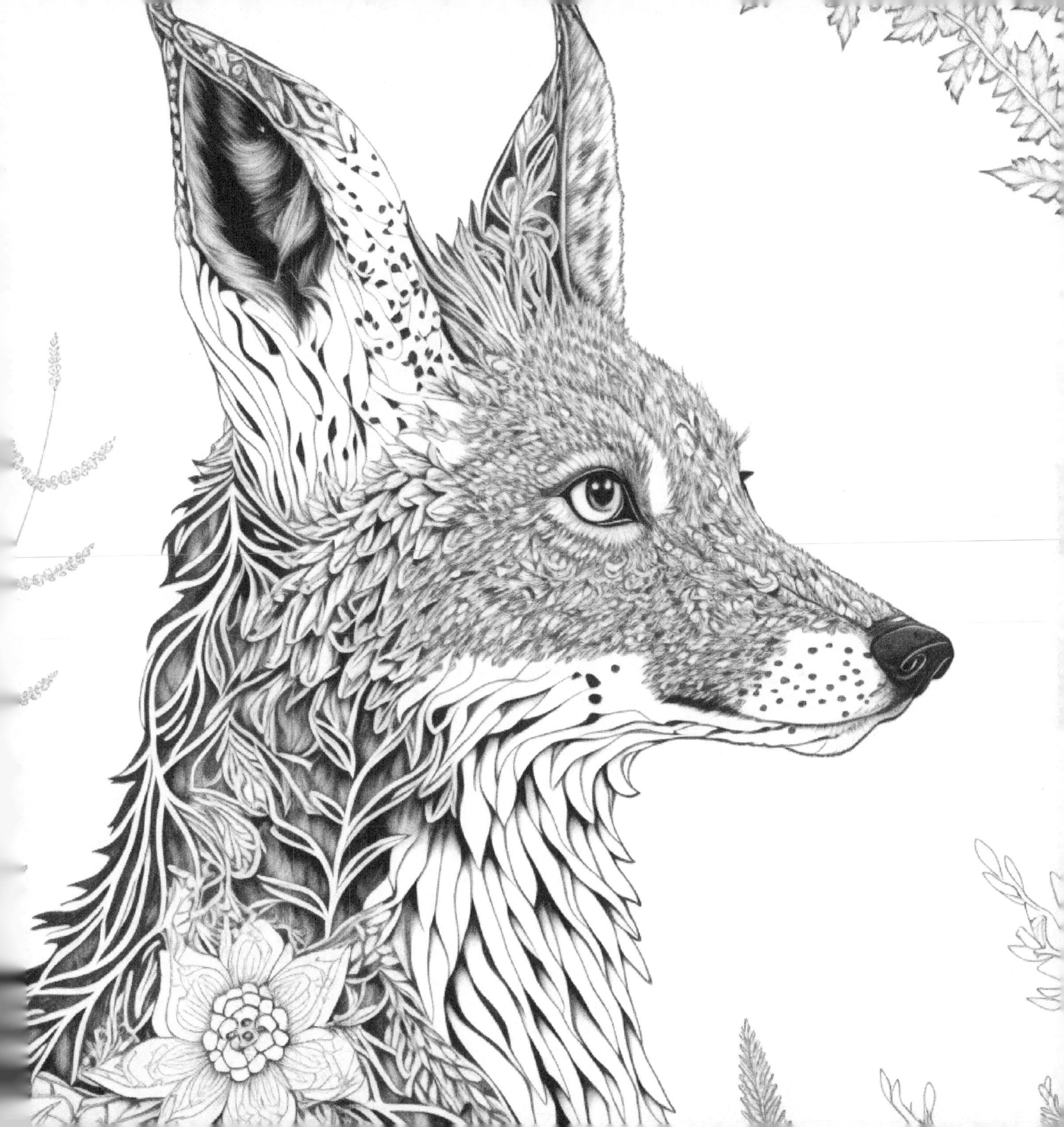

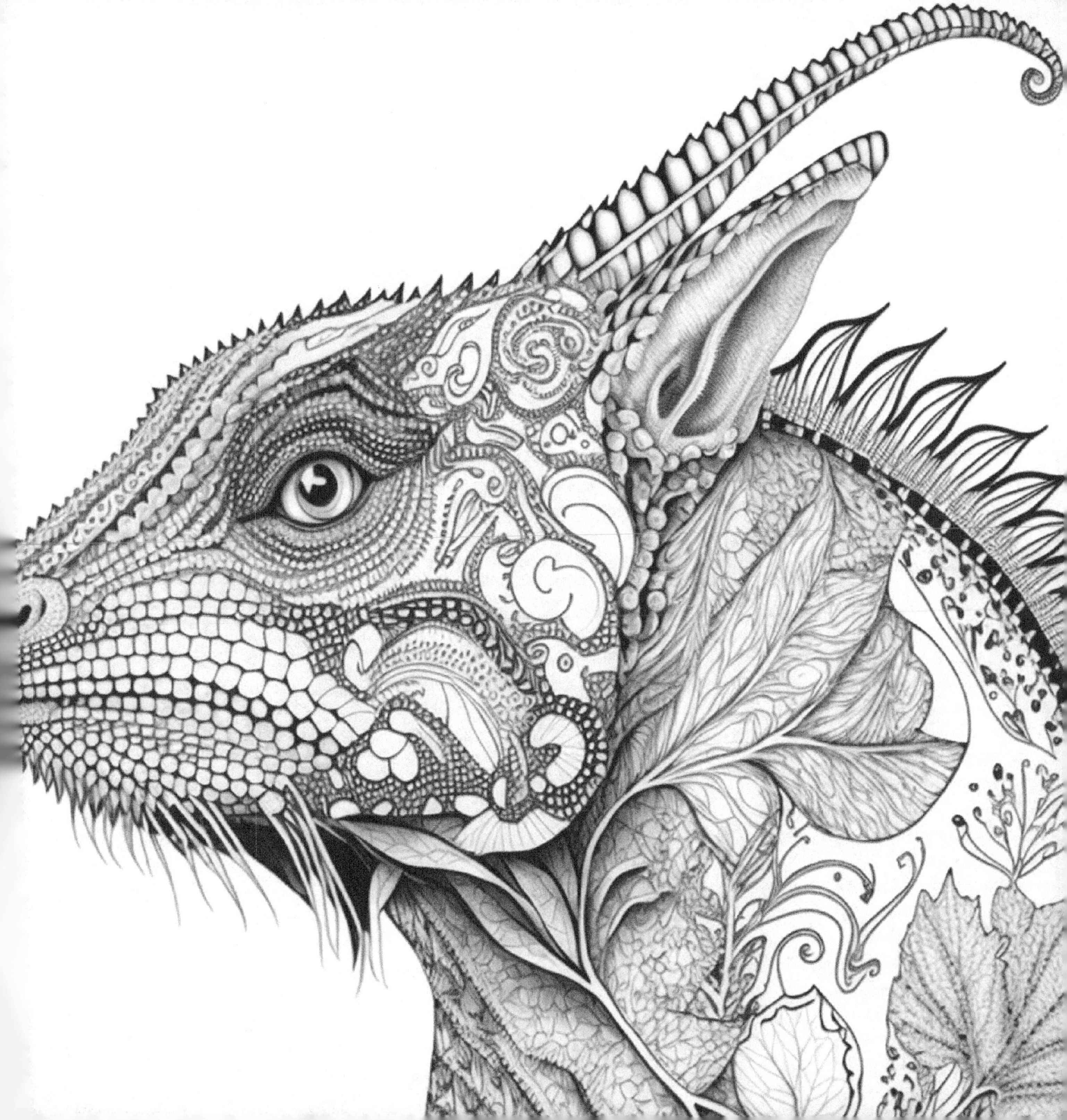

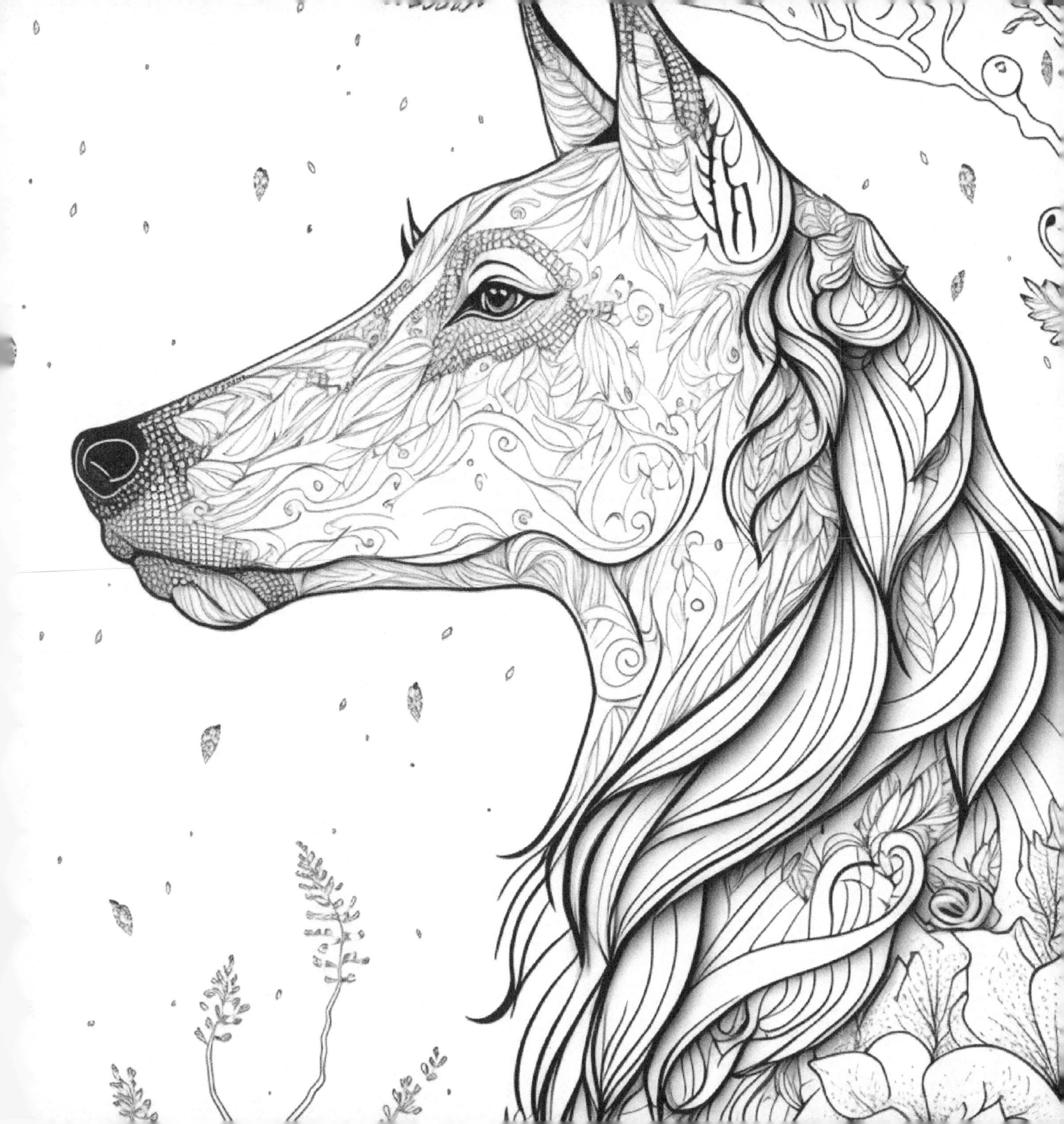

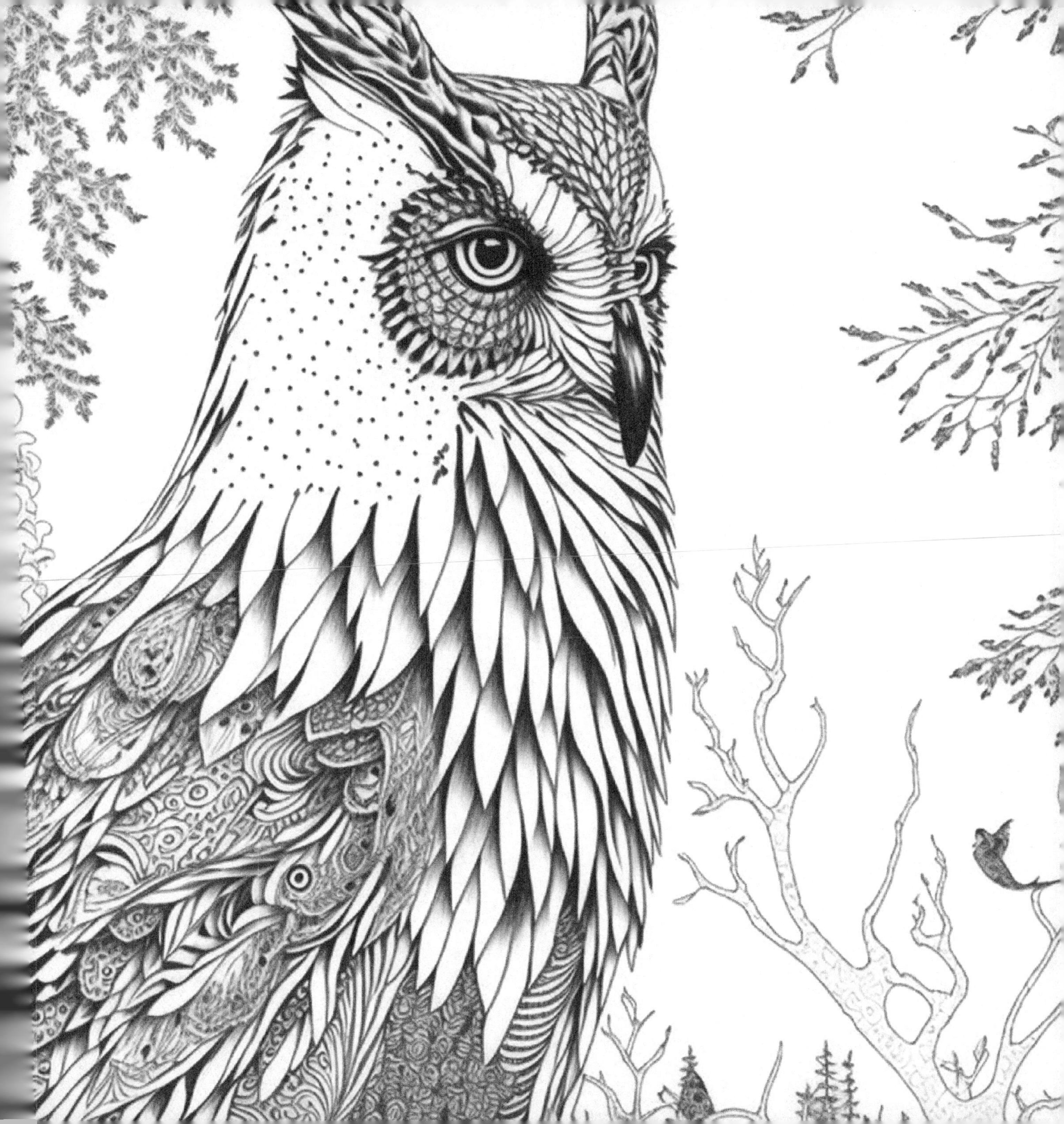

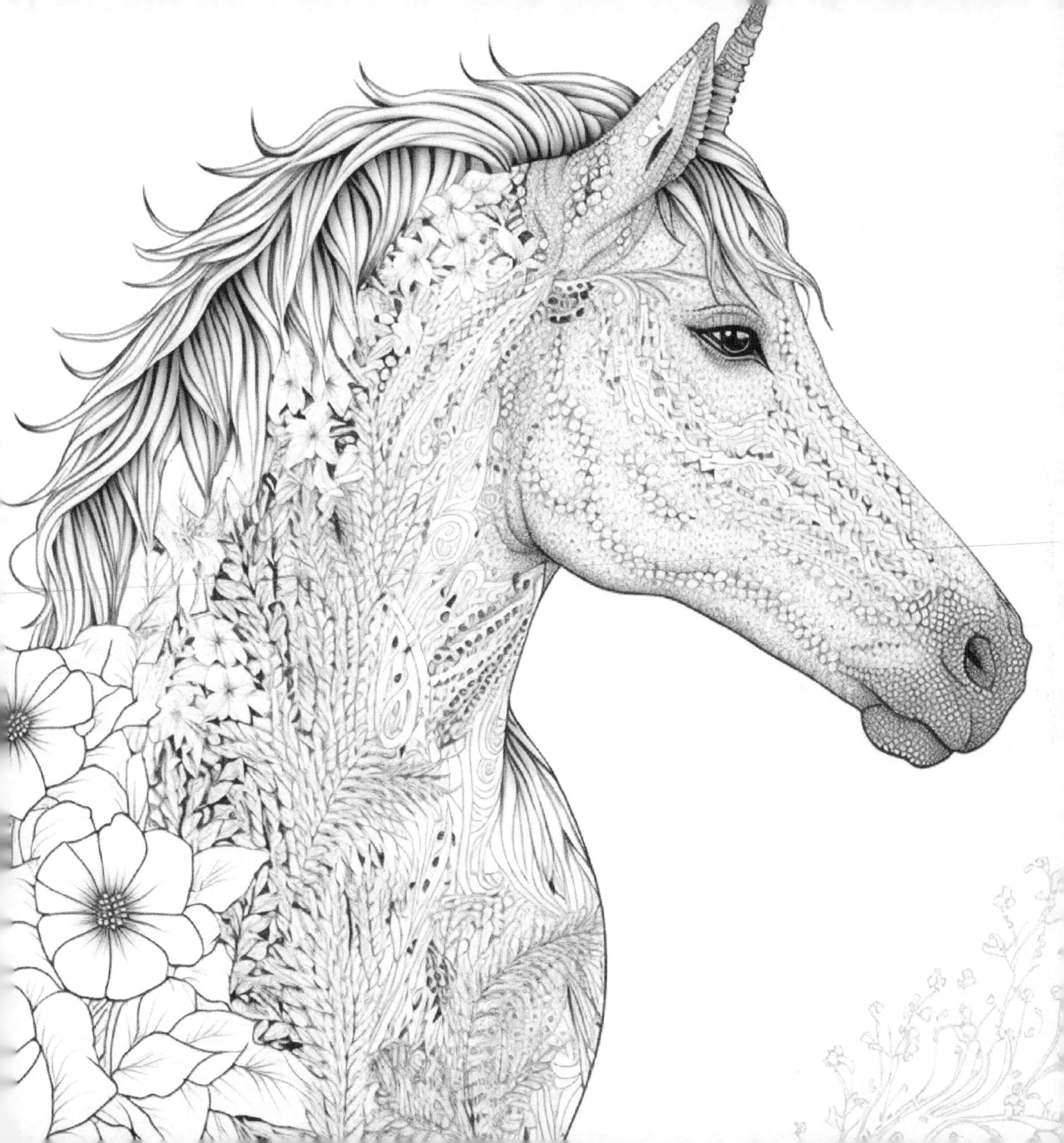

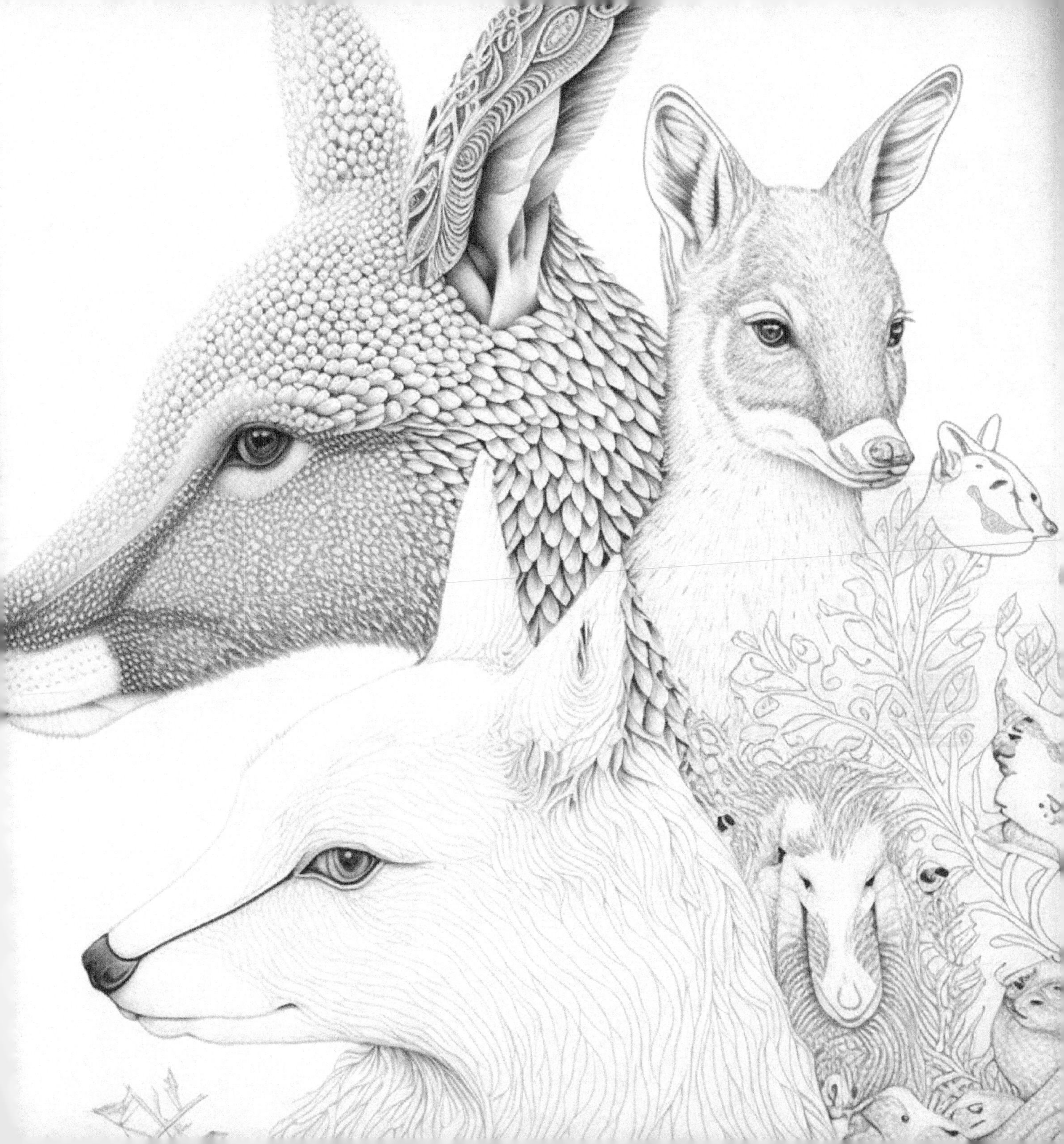

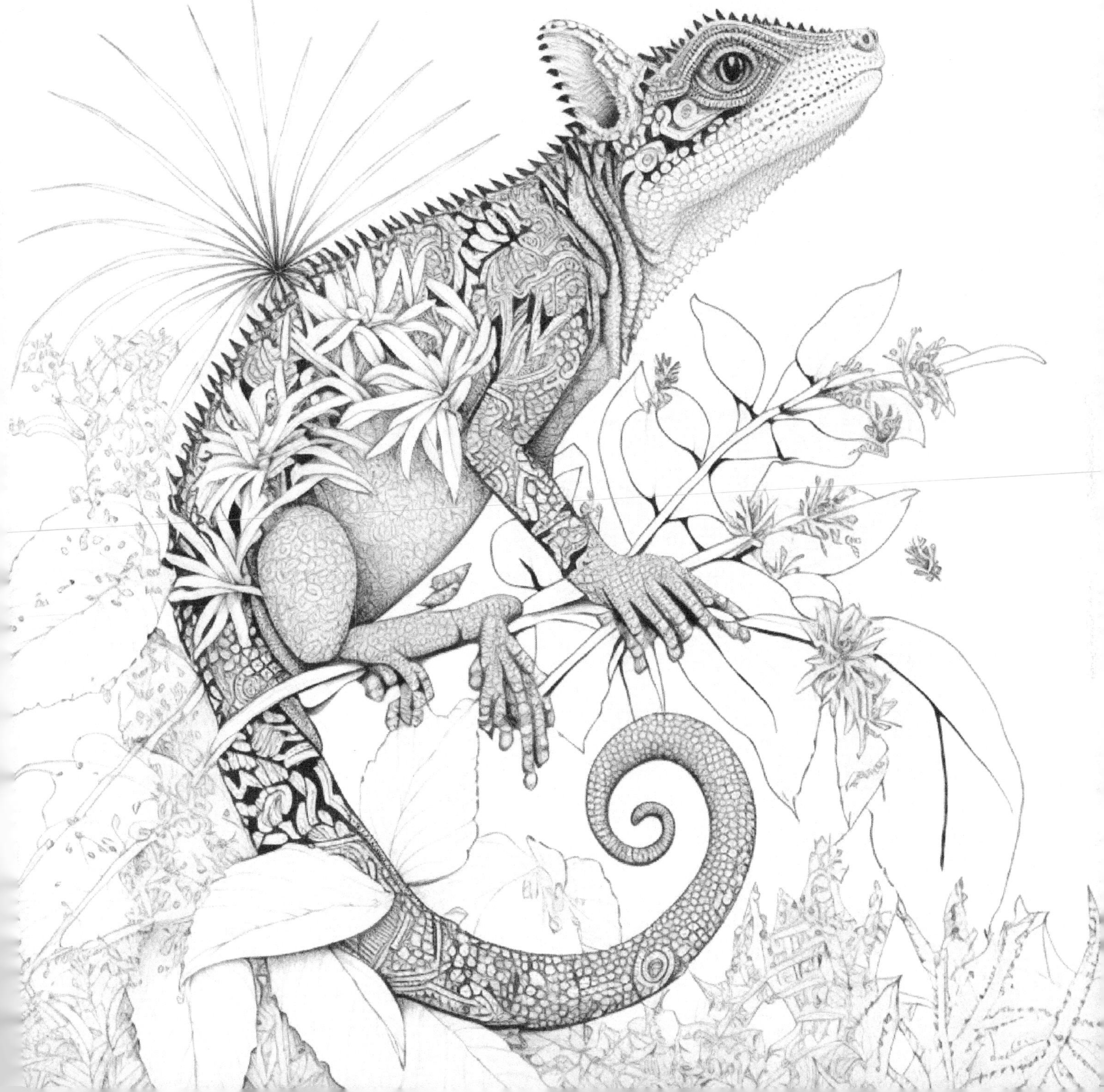

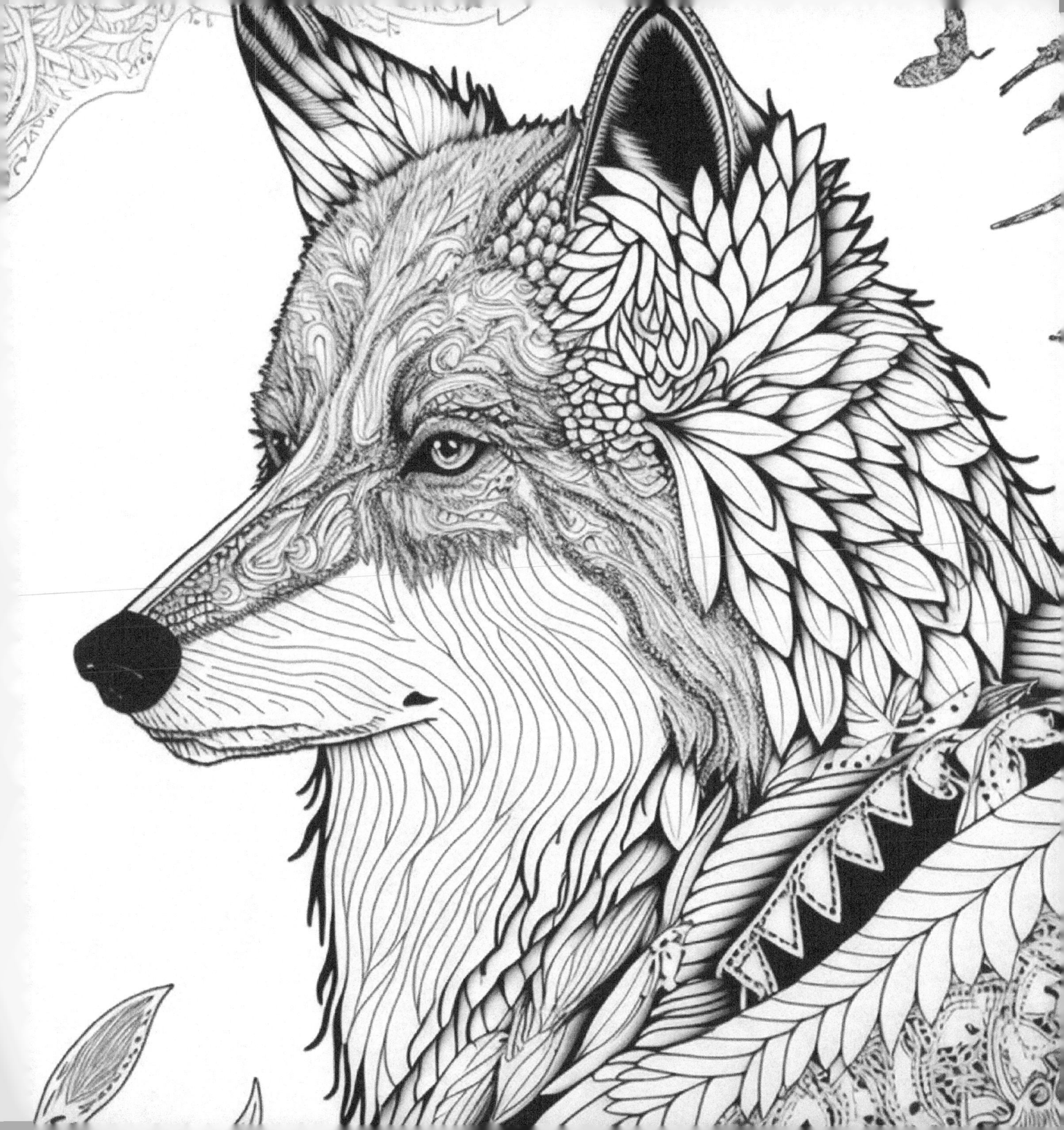

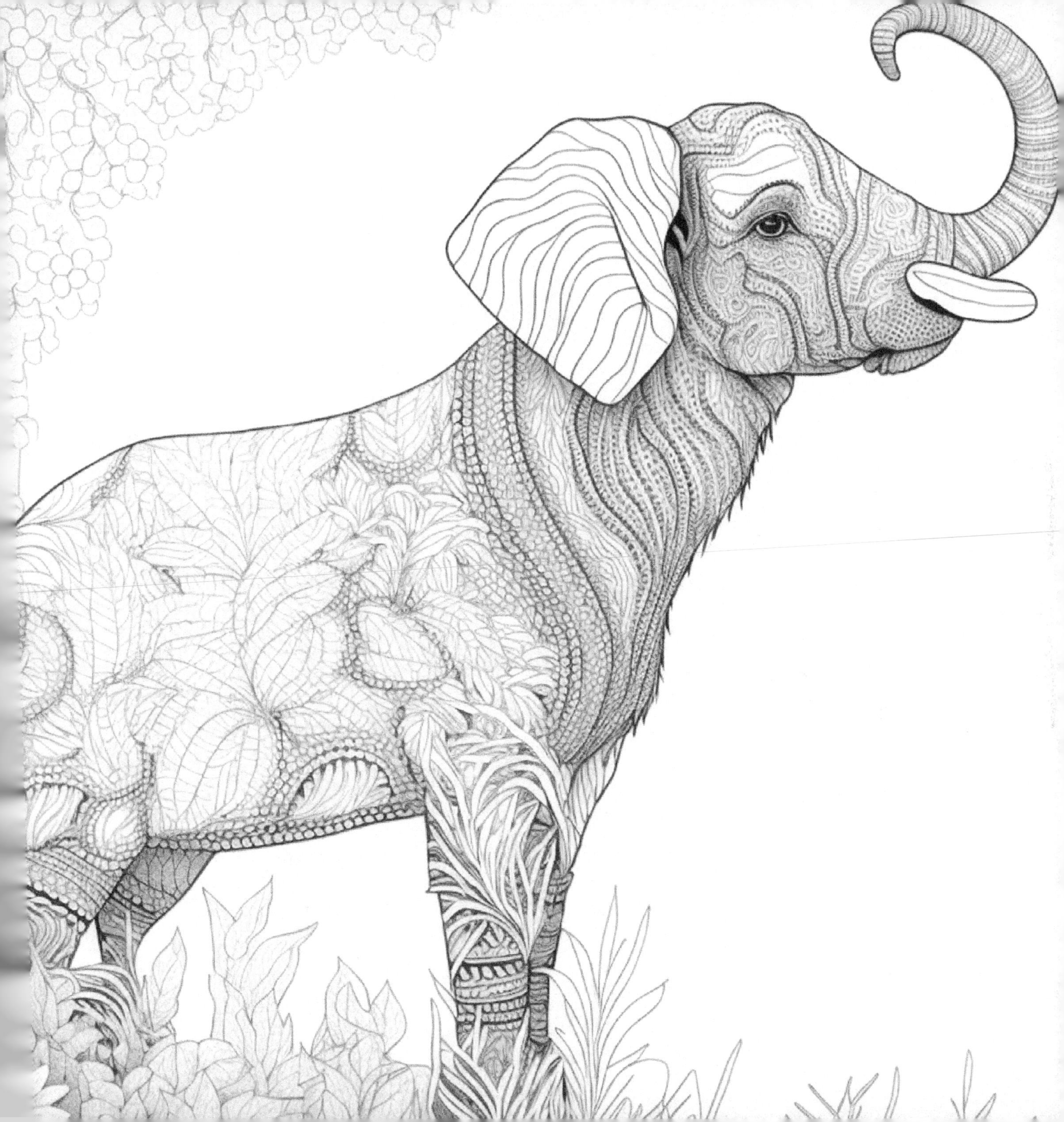

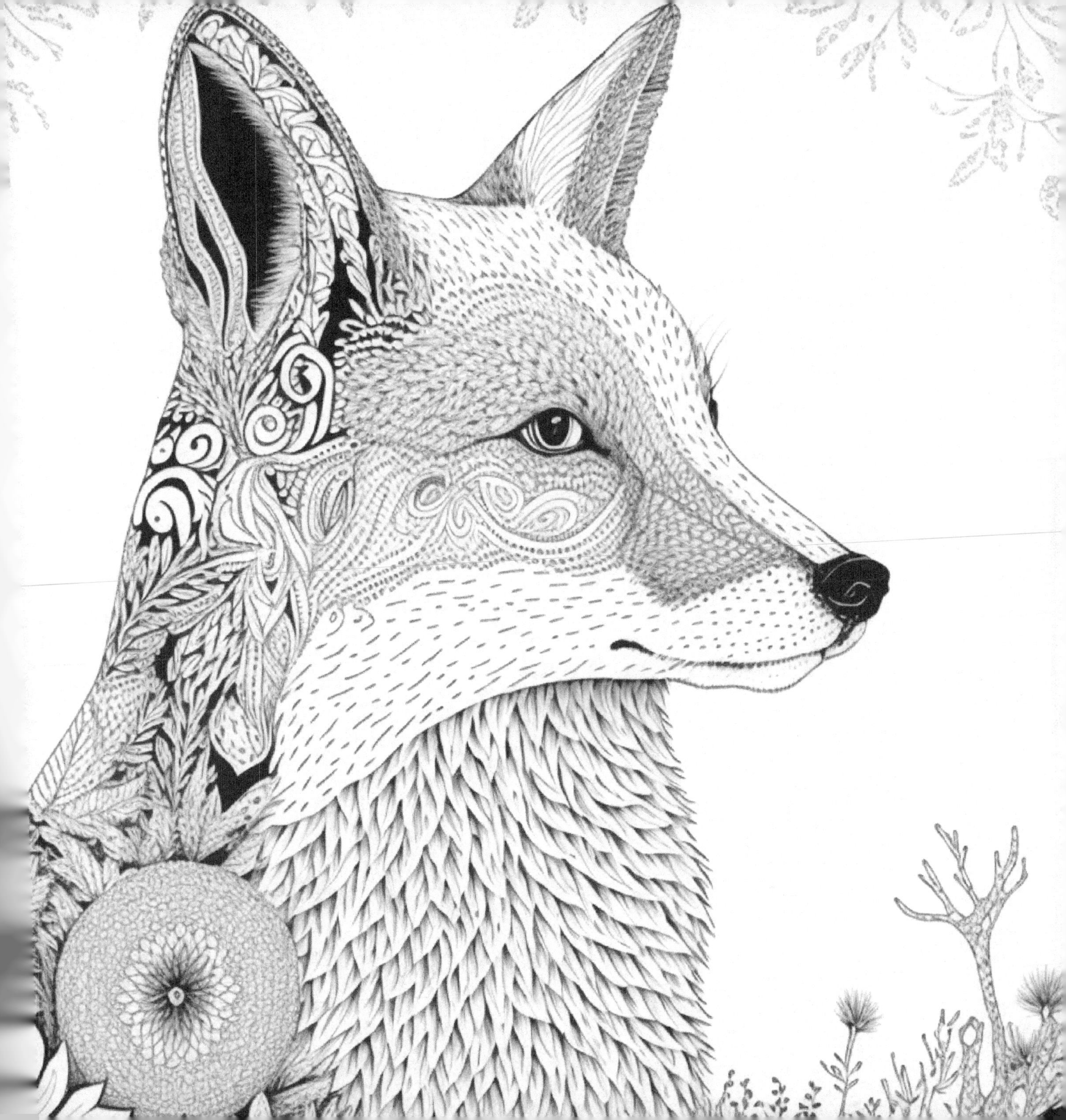

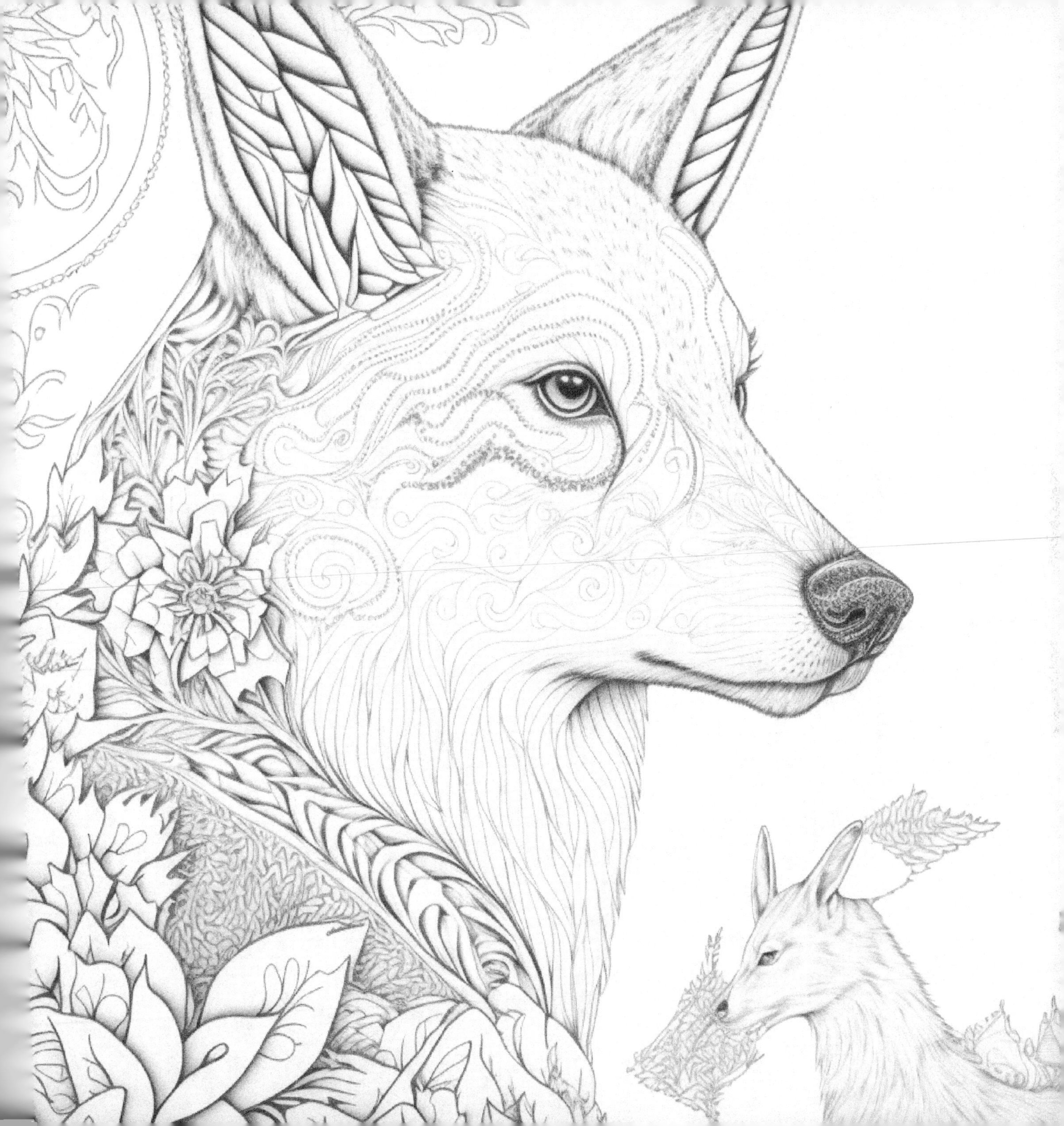

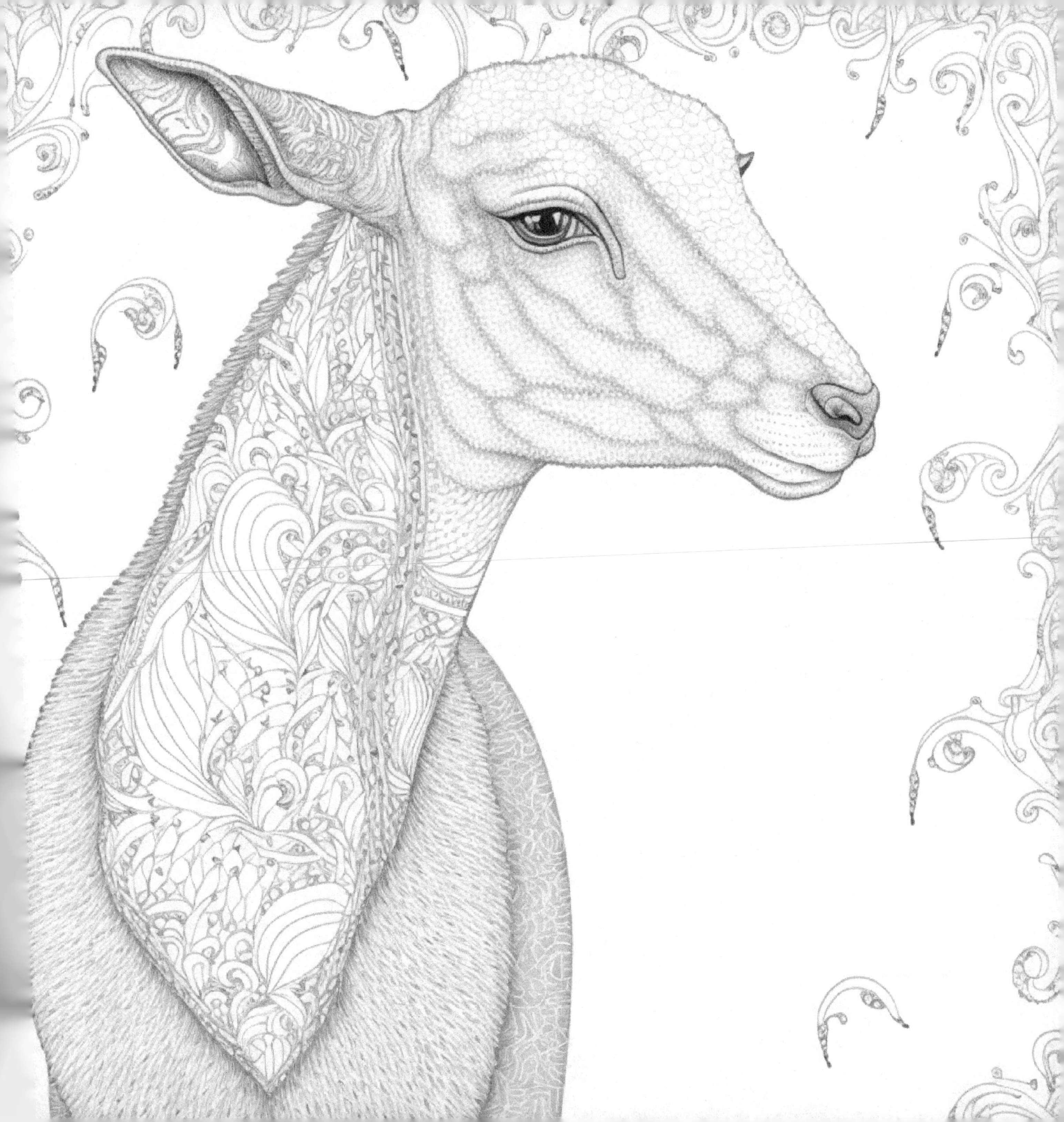

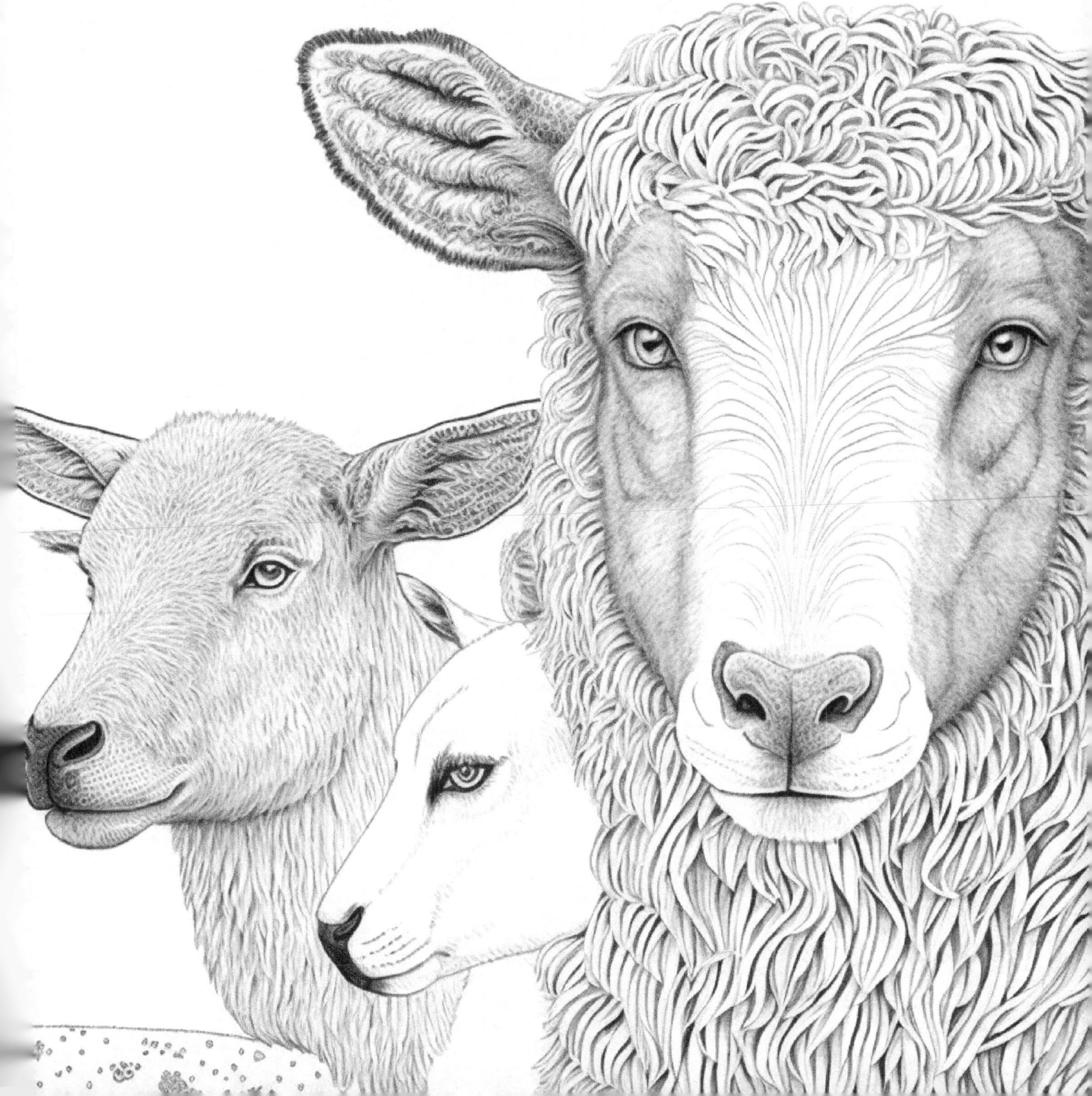

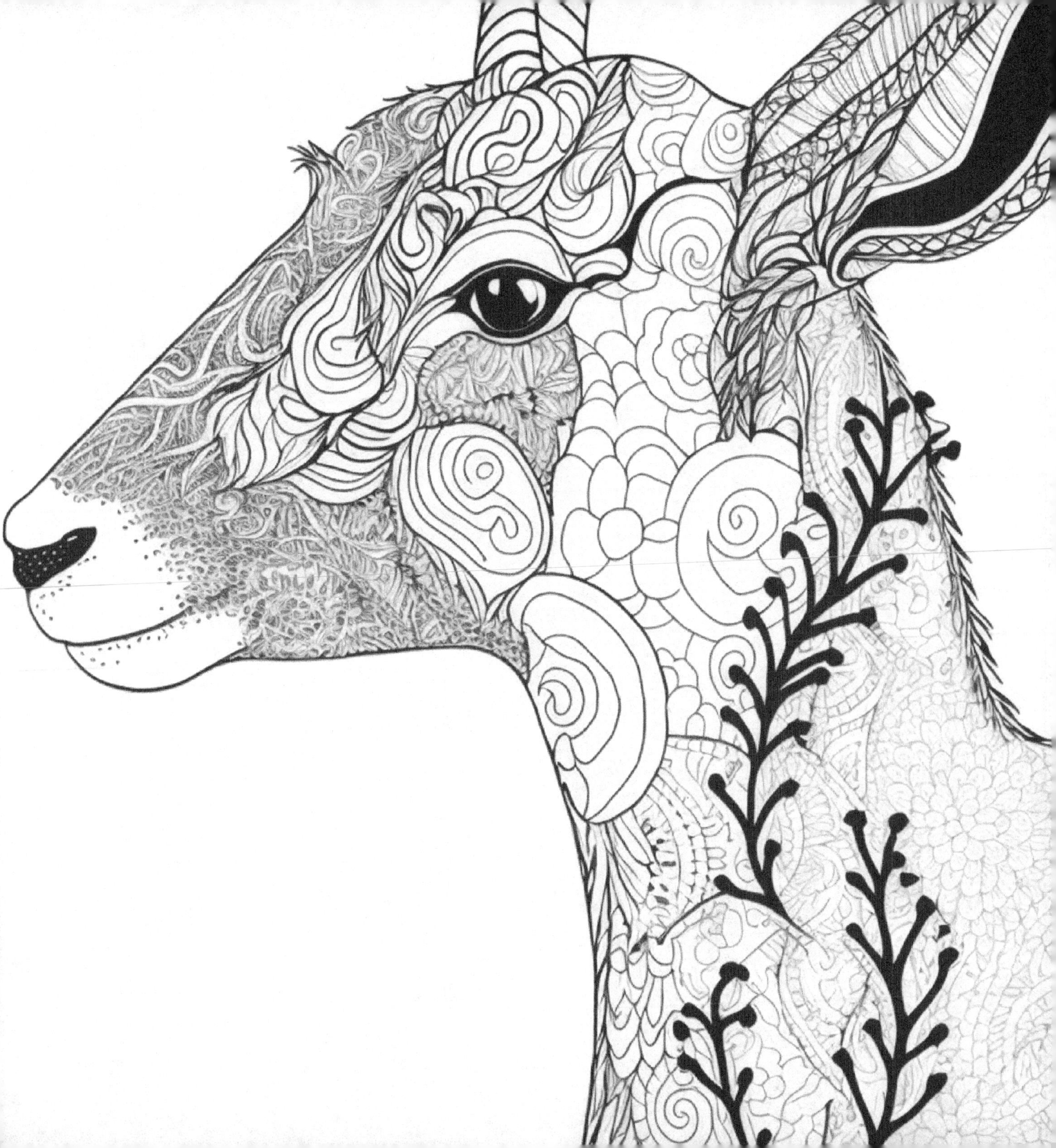

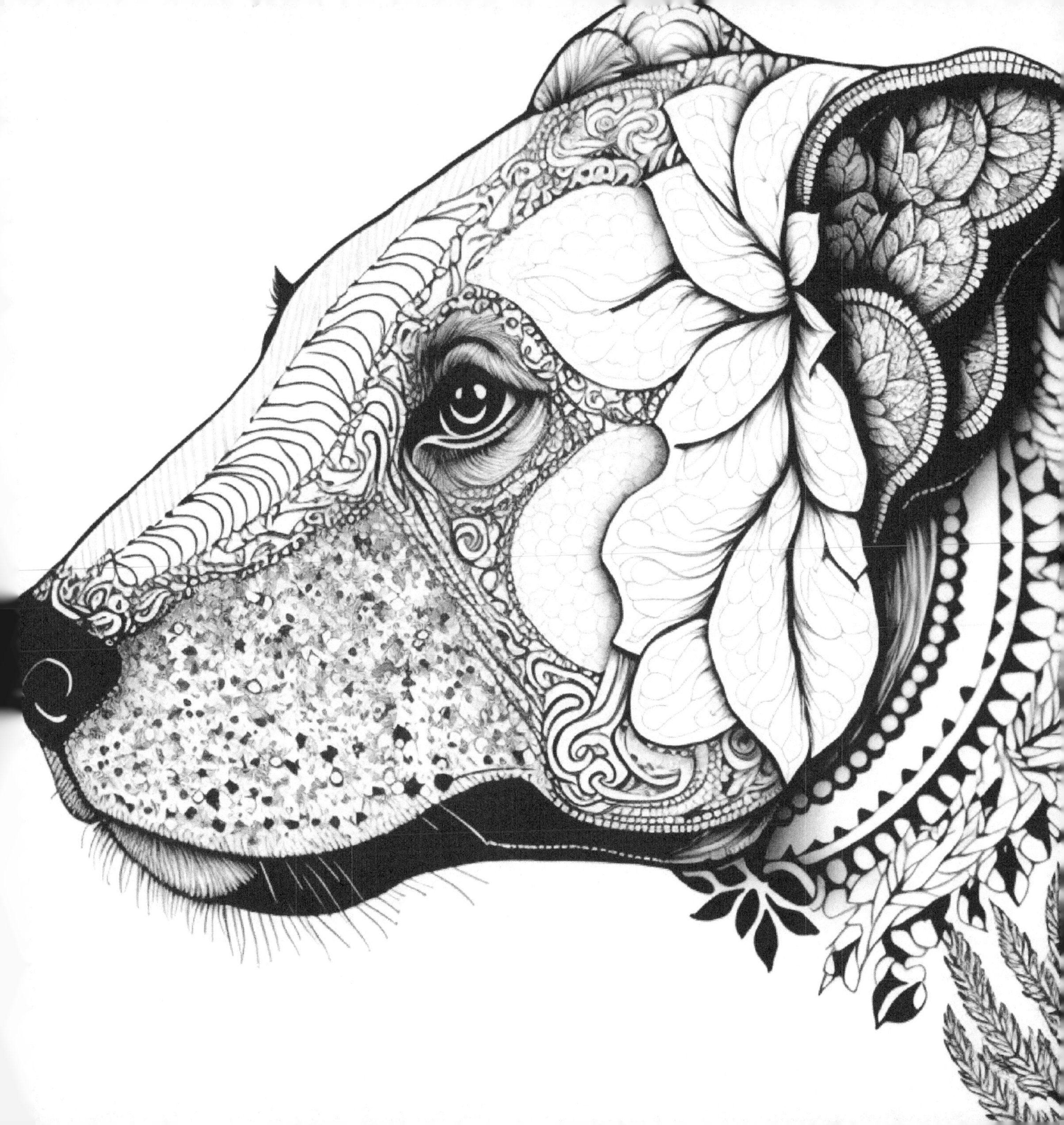

Please leave your feedback on Amazon if you enjoyed our book. Thank you!